TABLE OF CONTENTS

How To Monetize Social Trends
Yes, There Is Money To Be Made in Social Media
©Copyright 2013 by Dr. Noah Pranksky

Introduction – Social Media: The Lifeblood of Communication

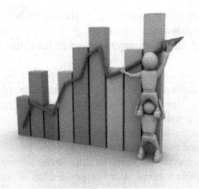

Ah...social media...the lifeblood of online communication! The net changes so rapidly today that it is more than a full time job just keeping up with the changes. Social media has exploded in 2011 and the changes affecting social media communication and engagement simply cannot be ignored.

Whether you use social media simply to communicate with family and friends or you use the commercial aspect of social media to engage customers, brand your products or utilize the eCommerce aspect of social media, it is important to watch the trends in order to provide a more personal and interactive experience for your customers.

Remember these two words – personal and interactive. These are the core values to social media for whatever levels of engagement you choose to use.

This year wasn't the first time any of us heard about the impact of social media on television. People have talked about TV shows on Facebook and Twitter for about as long as those social networks have existed, and the trend has only accelerated as social media usage in general has exploded.

Last year, chatter on Twitter helped the MTV Video Music Awards boost its audience to the biggest it had been in eight years. In 2011, services like Twitter and Facebook served as the virtual water cooler for just about every major news story and broadcast media event. It may not have been invented this year, but 2011 was pivotal for social TV.

American Idol was launched into the stratosphere using social media and text voting, both of which were never used before.

Twitter TV Grows Up

The events of 2011 - Revolution in Egypt, The death of Osama bin Laden, The launches of the iPad 2 and iPhone 4S, Amy Winehouse's death, The royal wedding, Losing Steve Jobs - a lot happened in 2011, but very little of it *didn't* unfold, at least in part, on the social Web.

The blending of media (trans-media) or the use of two or more media to report world events came of age in 2011. Twitter continued to be a driving force in the convergence of social media and television this year. With or without the encouragement of Twitter's management or TV networks, people would naturally be inclined to talk about shows in real-time on the Internet.

This fact has even helped the company start to carve out one viable idea for monetizing its service. Its social advertising products can let media companies tap into a passionate, pre-existing audience, gain more viewers and then get a rich and detailed amount of data back about how people responded to their campaign. Promoted tweets and topics aren't available exclusively for television shows, but the volume of TV-related chatter on Twitter, combined with the marketing budgets of TV studios and networks make it a win for both sides.

Twitter has further embraced its social role in TV, for example by teaming up with the creators of *X Factor USA* to implement live social voting mechanism for viewers to use during the program. To help encourage TV producers to get involved, Twitter published a best practices guide for integrating social media with television.

These social media-fueled discussions are more than just meaningless chatter. For those in the business of producing television shows, the phenomenon can be hugely valuable, with or without paying for social ads. This year, we saw more evidence of a positive correlation between Twitter buzz about a show and actual ratings.

Trends like this are not lost on digital marketers, who banded together this year to form the first trade group for advertisers and marketers looking to tap into future opportunities Internet-connected TVs.

Second Screen Apps, Content-Shifting and Tablet TV

The growth of tablets and smartphones is having a huge impact on television. About 86% of those who own such devices use it while they're watching TV, according to a study released by Yahoo in the beginning of the year. Many of them are tweeting and posting updates to Facebook about shows, while others are looking up pertinent information about programs they're watching. The proliferation of these devices has given rise to the growth of so-called second screen apps. This includes social check-in apps for entertainment such as GetGlue, which by September had seen an 800% increase in check-ins from the beginning of the year. Mind you, that was just before the Fall television season started.

Yahoo got in on the second screen app game this year by launching Yap.tv, a digital TV guide of sorts with Twitter integration and live chats and polls about television shows.

We're also beginning to see the early evolution of content-shifting for video and TV. Just as you can hit the "Read It Later" button for Instapaper, videos you come across during the day can be saved for later viewing as well. The "Later" button on all Vimeo players lets you save videos to a queue, while Boxee has its own bookmarklet for saving nearly any Web video to your Boxee account for later. It can be viewed from the desktop, of course, but perhaps more conveniently, the video will also appear immediately on Boxee's set-top box or its new iPad app. The app allows you to view saved videos, as well as browse a selection of videos shared by your Facebook and Twitter contacts, not unlike what Flipboard does for text-based content.

Watching TV content directly on tablets also grew more common this year. Apps like Hulu Plus and Netflix have been on the iPad since last year, but networks themselves are warming up to the idea of letting viewers catch up on their favorite shows on smaller screens. NBC released an iPad app that offers limited access to recent episodes, while HBO Go expanded its reach, although it's still only available to cable subscribers. Comcast subscribers can stream some content from the Xfinity iPad app, and the cable giant is even testing out live TV broadcasts over the Internet.

The future of TV is still very much emerging, but we fully expect 2012 to be another crucial year in its evolution. From Apple-branded TV sets to new (and quite possibly cheaper) tablets hitting the market in 2012, it will be interesting to see where things end up by this time next year.

Convergence Emergence - For a glimpse into how social will further integrate with "real life," we can look at what Coca Cola experimented with all the way back in 2010. Coke created an amusement park where participants could "swipe" their RFID-equipped wristbands at kiosks, which posted to their Facebook account what they were doing and where. Also, as part of a marketing campaign, Domino's Pizza posted feedback — unfiltered feedback — on a large billboard in Times Square, bringing together real opinions from real people pulled from a digital source and displayed in the real world. These types of "trans-media" experiences are likely to define "social" in the year to come.

The Cult of Influence - In much the same way that Google has defined a system that rewards those who produce findable content, there is a race on to develop a system that will reward those who wield the most social influence. One particular player has emerged, Klout, determined to establish their platform as the authority of digital influence. Klout's attempt to convert digital influence into business value underscores a much bigger movement which we'll continue to see play out in the next year. To some degree everyone now has some digital influence (not just celebrities, academics, policy makers or those who sway public opinion). But for the next year, the cult of influence becomes less about consumer plays like Klout and more about the tools and techniques professionals use to "score" digital influence and actually harness, scale, and measure the results of it.

Gamification Nation - No we're not talking about video games. Rather, game-like qualities are emerging within a number of social apps in your browser or mobile device. From levels, to leaderboards, to badges or points, rewards for participation abound. It's likely that the trend will have to evolve given how competition for our time and attention this gaming creates. Primarily, gamification has been used in consumer settings, but look for it in other areas from HR, to government, healthcare, and even business management. Perhaps negotiating your next raise will be tied to your position on the company's digital leaderboard.

Social Sharing - Ideas, opinions, media, status updates are all part of what makes social media a powerful and often disruptive force. The media industry was one of the first to understand this, adding sharing options to content, which led to more page views and better status in search results. What comes next in social sharing is more closely aligned with e-commerce or web transactions. For example, Sears allows a user to share a product or review with their networks directly from the site. Sharing that vacation you just booked, or recommending a product, or service from any site to a social network is where sharing goes next. We probably don't know what we are willing to share until we see the option to do it.

Social Television - For many of us, watching television is already a social act, whether it's talking to the person next to you, or texting, tweeting, and calling friends about what you're watching. But television is about to become a social experience in a bigger and broader sense. *The X Factor* now allows voting via Twitter and highlights other social promotions, which encourages viewers to tap social networks while they watch. Another way media consumption is becoming social comes from a network called GetGlue which acts as something of a Foursquare for media. Participants can "check-in" to their favorite shows (or other forms of media) and collect stickers to tell the world what programs they love. Watch for more of this, this year as ratings rise for socially integrated shows.

The Micro Economy - Lastly as we roll into 2012, watch for a more social approach to solving business problems through a sort of micro-economy. Kickstarter gives anyone with a project, the opportunity to get that initiative funded by those who choose to (and patrons receive something in return). A crowdsourcing platform for would be inventors called Quirky lets the best product ideas rise to the top and then helps them get produced and sold while the "inventor" takes a cut. Air BnB turns homes into hotels and travelers into guests, providing both parties with an opportunity to make and save money. These examples may point to a new future reality where economic value is directly negotiated and exchanged between individuals over institutions."

What does all of this mean for the arts community? Do you see other trends coming?

2011 is drawing to a close and with that naturally comes a new hype surrounding social media. So we'll now have a go at identifying what 2012 is likely to bring in the social mediasphere.

An important development we saw in 2011 was that more than 50% of businesses increased their social media spending and more than 1/3 of CEOs said social media was high on their business agenda (Booz & Company and Buddy Media's "Campaigns to Capabilities: Social Media and Marketing 2011" research).

Some things didn't go as planned, however – Facebook's location services (Places) did not really spark into life and has now evolved into a more sophisticated part of the status update. Will 2012 be the year of Google? Will Google+ stand toe-to-toe with Facebook or does it want to evolve into a highly complementary social search tool?

So while researching the web for this blog, the following topics kept on cropping up:

Social TV

More and more TV shows are including social media as part of the show's make-up. The X-Factor now allows voting through Twitter. And Sky Sports' Goals On Sunday has each presenter's Twitter handle under their name encouraging interaction and questions throughout the show to ensure that the topics discussed have been suggested by the viewers. Keep an eye out for companies using Facebook or Twitter to gain leads for their business. If you are a brand, you might want to start promoting your Twitter and Facebook pages wherever you can and work social media leads into your game plan for 2012.

F-commerce
It was pushed back and forth for a while but now it's safe to say that social media is here to stay in a business perspective. The figures quoted above are expected to grow significantly in 2012. Don't be surprised if you see a lot more social commerce (f-commerce) sites as opposed to simply branded pages where you interact with your favorite brands. Fans will soon become consumers and the sooner you make the leap, the better. A tool like Hubspot allows you to create a form to capture social media data, ensuring you turn those 'likes' into leads very easily. People are spending more time on social media sites and less time on the actual web as everything they need can be found within sites such as Facebook.

Branded Content
A great example of branded content, which is a mash-up of advertising and entertainment, is Red Bull's Art of Flight movie. It is essentially a snowboarding movie, backed by Red Bull and heavily endorsed with their brand logo. Nowhere in the film do they try to sell you any of their products but the association is so strong that if you love the film you'll almost feel an instant connection to the brand. Branded content comes in many forms but video, audio, graphics and blogs will be the crème de la crème as brands offer the consumer something more meaningful than competitions and promotions. Your Facebook, Twitter and YouTube fans will love this and they can be tied into a lead generation funnel simply by subscribing to your platform.

Social Search
Social search does exactly what it says on the tin – it searches social media platforms just like search engines do the internet. What makes social media so good is that it's full of opinions, ideas, and suggestions. With companies developing sites helping you share purchases with friends, or flag a holiday destination and ask for recommendations, social search is going to be a big player in 2012. Make sure you're interacting with your leads. If they are social searching, make sure you are too.

Social Gestures
Facebook's now introduced frictionless sharing, whereby actions on the social network are automatically shared without you having to hit a button (for reference, check out the Guardian's Facebook app where it tells your friends what you've read), 2012 will see more and more APIs based on social gestures. The ease of this function is there in the name – frictionless. You don't have to do anything at all for this to move to your networks. Love it or hate it, frictionless sharing is here to stay.

Eight social media trends you need to pay attention to for next year

2012 Social Media Trends

1. **Reporting to All Stakeholders**. Some countries, such as Australia, are reporting to all stakeholders. Meaning, they're not just doing investor relations, but reporting results to employees, customers, prospects, influencers, and more. This is going to become a bigger trend, especially as accounting principles are looking to include brand awareness as part of the balance sheet.

2. **Social TV Convergence**. I'm not a television watcher, but I'm seeing something interesting happening with apps, such as GetGlue. You can "check in" to a TV program and then have conversations with people around the world who are watching the same thing. It allows you to review the shows, talk about what's happening, and listen to what others are saying. It works for movies and music, too! Plus, if the rumors are true and Steve Jobs's last project *was* iTV, this will become HUGE next year.

3. **Integration of All Disciplines**. Integration is going to be crucial next year. Today we talk about mobile, social, marketing, public relations, advertising, direct, email, customer service, and sales as if they're working in silos. But 2012 is the year it needs to integrate. Customer service can't do its job without talking to sales. Sales need the help of public relations. And mobile can't live without marketing. You'll see these disciplines all work together, as if they're in a circle, and not in silos.

4. **Results**. If you aren't measuring your results to true dollars and cents, you may work yourself out of a job in 2012. We started to talk about how to do this earlier this month, but it's going to take learning some marketing, product management, and basic accounting (integration, integration, integration) to do this effectively.

5. **Email Marketing**. As much as I would love email to be dead, something like 107 trillion emails was sent in 2010. It's not going anywhere, yet most of us (as marketers) have forgotten about it. It's not the new, shiny penny and it's kind of old and stodgy (I think I read it's celebrating its 40th birthday). But it's still really effective. Everyone uses email. Not everyone uses social networks (yet).

6. **Social Commerce**. The other day I was in the Apple store and I checked in, using Foursquare. It asked me if I wanted to pay using the Apple app. Um, yes! Especially because it was a Sunday and there were a gazillion people there. So I downloaded the Apple app, scanned the mouse bar code, it gave me a subtotal, and I hit OK. It took the amount right out of my iTunes account, emailed me a receipt, and I was on my way. Starbucks does this using your phone and their at-register scanner. You'll see more and more of this next year.

7. **New Social Networks**. I know, I know. We need another social network like we need a hole in the head. BUT there are some cool things, such as Pinterest, that are gaining traction. In fact, yesterday I was scrolling through my Facebook stream and I saw Samuel Gordon Jewelers is having their first Pinterest contest: "Pin to Win." It's still way too early to see any results, but rest assured I'm watching what they're (and others) are doing with this and other new social networks.

8. **Print to Tablet Swap**. During the holiday weekend, I was scrolling through the app store on George (my iPad) and I found Catalogue. It stores all of your catalogs in a handy app so you can scroll through any of them at any time. It also recommends catalogs you should be reading, based on your preferences. My mom and I debated its merits the other day. She likes the tactile feel of turning the pages. I think it's super green and I love that I have them all in one spot. You'll see a big swap of print moving to the tablet in 2012.

Around this time of year we tend to see predictions from the cognoscenti (those in the know) about what will be hot in the coming year. I saw one today in the Huffington Post that caught my eye because I agree with the 4 trends Beverly Macy highlighted:

- The rise of Social Intelligence
- Better use of analytics and more focus on measurement
- Content curation
- Social media education and training

Social Intelligence

For several years now we've been told that at the very least we have to listen to the online conversations. The number of social media monitoring tools has exploded and at last count there were over 200 on the market. However, there is much more to be learned from these conversations than just brand mentions, complaints and sentiment.

Savvy PR and marketing folk are digging deep into the conversations – mining that data to find insights that can drive strategy, inform product R & D, give the competitive edge and improve that pesky bottom line.

You start by listening and gathering information about your brand/s, your company and your competitors. Once you have the data use that old PR skill called content analysis.

- Map your brand's social graph
- Find the influencers in each node of the graph
- Discover what different groups within one node are talking about and what's important to them
- Find out where they are talking about those things
- Tap into what your competitors are doing and what people are saying about them
- Identify threats and opportunities
- Share the data you find with your team and others across the organization
- Brainstorm how best to implement what you find to support the organization 's goals

There is a ton of information available in the social networks and conversations, but it takes commitment and work to find all the threads. A monitoring tool can do a lot of the work, but there is still a lot that has to be done manually. And the analysis cannot be done automatically. It takes a live person with a bright and inquiring mind to read the content and figure out what's important and what's connected. To see those brewing threats and spot the low-hanging fruit that will bring big rewards.

There is an old PR saying – "Know before you go."

For the past few years Social Media has been treated as a warm and fuzzy experiment. Now that we know it works, it's time to get serious about this data stream and use it to discover really useful information that can move the needle.

Social Media Intelligence is definitely a trend to watch in 2012

Learn how to do social audits and provide your company with the data they need to make the tough decision. It will definitely get the attention of the C-Suite and might even earn PR a seat at that elusive boardroom table.

Four social media trends predicted to be hot in 2012

- The rise of Social Intelligence

- Better use of analytics and more focus on measurement

- Content creation and curation

- Social media education and training

Social Media Intelligence is a sure bet in my view
Let's take a look at Analytics and Measurement.

Measurement

One of the aspects of social media that is changing as it matures is measurement When businesses first started to experiment with social media activity no-one was particularly concerned with measuring anything. Kind of like we found a new game of water polo, we all jumped in at the deep end, splashed around a lot and the more people in the pool and the more people we splashed, the better. We were playing the game, but we weren't too sure who was on our team or where the goals were. But since everyone else was there, it seemed like we should be too.

Social media is no longer a game or an experiment. It's an accepted and effective business strategy. It is on the CEO's radar. According to a report by Useful Social Media, 12% of the companies surveyed claimed that social media was under the direct control of the CEO.

There is certainly an increased pressure on corporate social media practitioners to deliver on investment – there's an ever more pressing need to demonstrate ROI, along with progress against other crucial KPIs. But this simply represents social media being treated as a regular business investment, says the report.

74% of CMOS (chief marketing officers) agree that social efforts were finally tied to hard ROI.
What are they measuring?

Some of these are outputs and outtakes, but a good number of them are outcomes: what did people do as a result of reading your content or engaging with you on a social site?

Did they click a link, share your content, visit a landing page, fill in a form, download a whitepaper or a coupon, watch a video or recommend you to a friend?

CMOs are also measuring purchases and customer satisfaction via reduced returns, lower call center volume and fewer complaints.

One measurement that rarely gets mentioned in these studies is amplification. We know that word of mouth is powerful and it's even more so on social media. When a friend shares something with you it has a much deeper affect than if you received it from the brand.

It is possible to measure how many times your message gets shared by your fans and followers in Facebook and Twitter and it gives you a good measure of the success of your social content. It also highlights brand affinities and identifies your brand advocates.

Analytics

This is an area that traditionally has not been a PR skill, but it is one we have to master. And we need to do it in a hurry!

Several years ago Jim Sterne of the Web Metrics Summit said that someone who can understand web analytics and interpret the numbers for the marketing and PR people is worth their weight in gold – and I believe that is still the case today.

So how can you measure all these items? What tools can you use?

Start by learning the basics of Google Analytics.

Facebook Insights has a fairly robust set of analytics.

TweetReach is a good tool for tracking amplifiers in Twitter.

Although measurement, statistics and analytics have not been top of the list of PR skills in the past, they are going to become more and more important going forward. It's no surprise to me that they are on the list of hot trends for 2012.

At the end of each and every year, we tend to look back and try to identify the most significant events that recently emerged so we can predict trends that will continue to grow well into the New Year and reshape social media.

There's a lot to take into account and nobody could ever accurately predict what will happen in the future, but it's interesting to try anyway. Here are a few social media predictions we are expecting to see in 2012.

A bigger shift in social media toward branding, customer service and B2B marketing

It has become increasingly more important for businesses to invest in social media for promoting their products or services and for communicating with customers. In time, businesses won't be able to afford NOT to use social media for marketing.

In 2012, more businesses should be paying closer attention to blog posting, content marketing and interacting with customers through networks like Facebook and Twitter.

Of course, while social media has always traditionally been embraced by the B2C (business-to-consumer) sector, it's also expected that B2B (business-to-business) branding through social media will experience significant growth 2012.

Relevant and measurable social media influence

Social media influence has been a touchy subject in 2011, especially after Klout changed their scoring algorithm. Some people argue that you simply can't measure a person's true influence with a number, while others say that social influence measurement will continue to play a large role in an individual or company's social media activity.

It may be long after 2012 when we see a real, significant impact by the measurement of social influence given that social influence is in its "embryo" stage. Still, sites like Klout, Kred and PeerIndex should continue to grow in popularity and complexity throughout the New Year.

Social television converging with traditional television

Don't be surprised to see traditional TV and the internet converge and reshape the way we choose how, when and why we watch television in 2012.

It sounds like Apple will be launching a new product or service involving television in the near future, and we already love using Internet services like Hulu, Netflix, YouTube and others to watch our favorite shows on demand.

In 2012, it looks like all of our media devices including our television sets, computers, laptops, tablets, and smartphones could come together to offer us more social and sharable television experiences that we can enjoy whenever we want.

Social media affecting search results.

Search engines like Google are continuously perfecting their algorithms, and they'd be out of their minds to ignore the shift toward social media relevance. Google recently made some tweaks to their search algorithm that now returns timelier and recently published content in search results.

For websites and companies that have blogs updated frequently, the integration of social media into search engine results is important. Moreover, search results are getting a lot more personal and customized to individual preferences, especially now with the integration of Google+.

Pages that have previously been shared by your network on Facebook, Twitter or Google+ rank higher in your own search results. However, for somebody else's search results for the same keyword may look comparably different because their network of friends shares different content.

Expect to see your search results move even more toward social relevance in 2012.

Facebook taking sharing to a whole new level

At the time of this writing, Facebook has not yet fully rolled out its new Timeline profile to all users and people still have to press the "like" button manually to share content with their friends on Facebook.

Eventually, Facebook sharing will become automatic. When you're reading a blog post on your favorite blog or watching a YouTube video from one of your favorite creators, it will be shared automatically via open graph sharing.

To sum it up, Facebook is way ahead of all the other social networks out there and will likely become the web's default sharing platform in the coming years. Get ready to see those huge changes (including automatic sharing) start to roll out in 2012.

As the end of the year draws near, it's time to start looking at social media trends for 2012. Businesses should get ready for seismic shifts on the digital landscape.

Competition will intensify as the rules of marketing are further altered by social media, mobile web and all in real-time. For businesses that don't start embracing social media, 2012 may mark the beginning of their declining growth and profit.

According to Nielsen's "The Social Media Report," social media use is commonplace, with over 4 to 5 Internet users engaging in social activity across a wide variety of platforms. Social networks and blogs are the top online destinations, accounting for 23% of time Americans spend online. Pew Internet and American Life Project's August 2011 report states that nearly two-thirds (65%) of all adult Internet users now use social networks. The skyrocketing growth of social media has broad implications–beyond consumer behavior.

While some businesses are evolving or even transforming how they buy and sell products, many are fast becoming social businesses. In a *Fast Company* article by Drew Neisser, *"Move Over Social Media; Here Comes Social Business"* he explains the reasons why every company should be thinking about becoming a *social business*. According to Neisser, IBM is moving themselves and their clients "well beyond social media into a new era of collaboration, insight sharing and lead generation it calls social business".

One of the hottest business social trends in 2011, leveraged by both large and small size businesses, has been *social commerce*. Social Commerce is essentially word-of-mouth applied to e-commerce. According to Brian Solis, "Social Commerce is rising quickly, but this isn't a story about technology, it's a story about how and why people make decisions." Take a look at this amazing Infographic Social Commerce Timeline created by Useful Social Media that depicts the evolution of this new process. Social Commerce is redefining the way brands and consumers interact.

One of the best examples of Social Commerce is the mobile YP.com app which lets you share deals with family and friends via Facebook, Twitter, email and SMS. According to David Williams, vice-president of product management at AT&T Interactive, "Gas is just one of many everyday essentials where a few simple factors: location, price and brand, brought together in a thoughtful design can help direct users toward smarter choices and quicker decisions."

The process for migrating from social media to social business will vary depending on the nature, size and strategy of your business. But you should be aware of some of these emerging social trends and tools as you consider how to capitalize on opportunities and achieve your business goals.

[building communities, brands, mobile, etc.]?

I posed this question to several industry experts (crowdsourced the community) and here is what they had to say:

...for building communities?

"Businesses are more and more looking at social media marketing as a strategic business driver now, so you'll see a lot more insistence on accountability, measurement and quantification of what social media means for companies. From a community building standpoint, that means community managers are going to be challenged to delineate the value of those community members versus non-community members, make logical arguments for why and how a community's growth is positive for the business and illustrate how they affect the bottom line revenue of a company. It's going to challenge many to think beyond the comment, like and fan. But it will make us all better."

...for brands?

"2012 will be characterized by a far greater number of brands embracing purpose as a strategy to be meaningful to their media savvy and connected customer communities. The most sophisticated brands will focus their attention on increased transparency and accountability inspiring their community to see themselves as partners in the brand's success and positive social impact. Those that continue to resist the business implications of social technology will quickly lose market share and disappear as the same dynamics playing out in the political sphere around the world become commonplace in the private sector."

...for mobile?

"In 2012, mobile will move to center stage in social, as everyone has a phone, with close to a majority of those being smartphones. Location-based messaging between people, and especially between people and businesses of all sizes, will increasingly be initiated by individuals as they tap into their personal networks and networks of those around them to seek and share information. Besides being highly personal, mobile will become the social conduit."

...for customer service?

"In 2012, more companies will consider use of social monitoring and analytics to help them understand sentiment, key influencers and the types of people chatting about their brand. In addition, growth of the social space will raise the importance of dialog between customer service groups and social media teams. This improved collaboration can lead to an integrated plan to better handle inquiries via the various channels."

...for crowdsourcing?

"2012 will be the year that "Crowdsourcing" stops becoming a buzzword and starts becoming one of the most cost effective ways for small to medium sized business to engage their stakeholders. The term too often associated with contests, is actually a reliable means of message virality and real-time engagement. Marketing, customer service, sales, and PR can all be given a huge boost through the use of their crowd, especially via their social media platforms."

...for small businesses?

"Biggest trend in social media for small business? One that has already started but now many are getting the fruits of their labor: networking. Finding each other to share stories and learning. Finding talent to join the business. Finding prospects to try to convert to customers. For networking, social media is the small business owners' best friend."

...for retail?

"With the advent of in-network apps like Spotify, Hulu and Netflix directly within Facebook, users are going to rapidly gain a sense of comfort with the idea of Facebook as a marketplace. In 2012, the trend will be toward the addition of other non-digital shopping apps on Facebook, allowing consumers to literally buy goods and services directly from their Facebook Timeline. Things like gym memberships, vacations, cleaning services and more will become available on Facebook."

...for B2B?

"2012 will further separate the pretenders from the purposeful. B2B marketers that don't take ownership of social media as part of a strategic inbound engine will be an endangered species by the end of 2012. Small businesses will realize Social Media is far from free and the trend will be serious budget increases for creating content, automating tools, and the human resources to sufficiently scale engagement with their marketplace."

...for technology?

"In 2012, marketing technology will continue to converge. We'll see social media features embedded into more products, from CRMs and marketing automation systems to web content management and landing page optimization platforms. These technologies that reach deeper into the customer experience lifecycle will reveal more nuanced metrics for tying social influence to business value. Likes, follows, and +1's will be more meaningful in the context of specific customer experiences rather than an abstract performance measurement unto themselves."

...for marketing?

"'The social media trend for business in 2012 will be less media or marketing and more social. Social media will move beyond marketing, PR and customer service and will become an extension of an entire businesses employee, customer and partner base. Real-time response management, tracking and alerts will be the tools of choice. Response managers will be on the hiring plans of many more companies and social selling will begin to become a reality in many more organizations. In effect, we will start to see businesses truly engaging with the market in a people-to-people model."

...for SEO?

One key trend for social media and SEO in 2012 will be resonance. A resonant piece of content (blog post, video, infographics, etc.) combines quality research and thought with an issue that prospective customers really care about (e.g., using technology to better engage buyers early in their buying process). Resonant content is more likely to be read, shared and commented upon. That sharing across social media sites and networks in turn will drive search traffic to the content, further increasing its reach and impact. Companies will need to do keyword research in addition to experimentation with different messages in order to determine which phrases and concepts truly resonate with their audiences.

...for advertising?

"Social media is truly now the mainstream media. So one of the big trends next year is that social will continue to become nearly everyone's primary source of content and interaction. Because of this, we will see early adopters who have learned along the way to make their advertising content relevant and interesting finding that it becomes easier and easier to ride this trend and get their customers to pass content along for them. Of course like any successful marketing campaign if that content accurately reflects the strategic business objective, it's a huge win with positive long-term implications."

...for PR?

"Social Media for PR is evolving from a listening post and ratings game to a strategic tool that provides insight and analytics into customers, prospects, competitors and thought leaders. Never before have PR practitioners had the opportunity to gain real-time insight into customer, prospect and competitor behavior and be able to shape conversations based on that data. We will see more data crunching and analysis and more strategic and targeted responses. As more and more content moves to mobile, we will also see more creative uses of content, more app development and more use of the comment function for thought leadership. New forms of press releases optimized for mobile readers will evolve. PR will also embrace new types of content marketing geared to mobile. All in all, it will be a productive time as PR rises to meet the technological opportunities."

Resources

Air BnB
Boxee for iPad
Catalogue
Flipboard
Foursquare
GetGlue
Hulu Plus
HBO Go
Instapaper
Kickstarter
Klout
KRED
PeerIndex
Pinterest
Quirky
Red Bull's Art of Flight
Spotify
TweetReach
Yap.tv
YP.com App
Xfinity

*****

About the Author:

Dr. Noah Pranksky is a research behavioral scientist for Applied Mind Sciences. His research involves many aspects of the human mind including relationships, energy psychology, and various protocols and modalities relating to treatment and cure of various mental maladies.

He and his wife Marianne reside in Portland, Oregon.

Visit some of his websites

http://www.AddMeInNow.com
http://www.AppliedMindSciences.com
http://www.BookbuilderPLUS.com
http://www.BookJumping.com
http://www.EmailNations.com
http://www.EmbarrassingProblemsFix.com
http://www.ePubWealth.com
http://www.ForensicsNation.com
http://www.ForensicsNationStore.com
http://www.FreebiesNation.com
http://www.HealthFitnessWellnessNation.com
http://www.Neternatives.com
http://www.PrivacyNations.com
http://www.RetireWithoutMoney.org
http://www.SurvivalNations.com
http://www.TheBentonKitchen.com
http://www.Theolegions.org
http://www.VideoBookbuilder.com

**Some Other Books You May Enjoy From
ePubWealth.com, LLC Library Catalog**

EPW Library Catalog Online
http://www.epubwealth.com/wp-
content/uploads/2013/07/Leland-benton-private-turbo.pdf

EPW Library Catalog Download
http://www.filefactory.com/f/562ef3ea1a054f0a

www.ingramcontent.com/pod-product-compliance
Lightning Source LLC
Chambersburg PA
CBHW070929050326
40689CB00015B/3683